PRESENT YOUR BEST

How to deliver high impact training

BRIAN WARD

Published 2019

By Million Dollar Author

Copyright © 2019 by **Brian Ward**

All rights reserved. No part of this publication may be reproduced, distributed or transmitted in any form or by any means, without prior written permission.

Million Dollar Author publishing
Sydney, Australia

Book Layout © 2019 Business Growth Advisors
Editing Grace Evelyn

Present your best by Brian Ward. -- 1st ed.
ISBN 978-0-9943007-8-2

Don't die with any fun in the bank

—BRIAN WARD

ABOUT THE AUTHOR

Husband and life partner to Shell, Father of Billy and Frazer, lover of life and having as much fun as possible whilst on this beautiful planet.

Brian's career has spanned some 40 years from joining the RAF at 17 years old in 1979 and then serving 23 years. Emigrating to New Zealand joining the RNZAF at the ripe age of 41 and serving a further 13 years, before emigrating to Australia and finally starting his own business BRIAN 8 at the age of 54. Brian has spent some 26 years in the training arena and has taught subjects from Aircraft Engineering through to Emotional Intelligence and building high performance teams. His style is fun and engaging, his passion and enthusiasm are limitless, he is one of the few who are gifted with pure creative thought.

"I've now got to the point in life where I think I should unload and share the training knowledge inside my head, because it's been filling up for the last 26 plus years."

CONTENTS

TRAINING DOESN'T NEED TO BE BORING.......9
NEVER LEAVE A SOLDIER BEHIND 13
ACCELERATED LEARNING 19
   It's o.k. to say I don't understand 22
FINDING A MORE EFFECTIVE WAY 25
   Another way...25
   Creating a good environment for learning............26
   The Present your best model.................................38
UNWRAPPING THE MODEL 41
   Laughter helps you learn.......................................45
   Throw out the old rule book..................................47
   Creating an Adult learning environment...............48
   Buy-in 52
   Fun and Activity 56
3 FRUSTRATIONS OF TRAINING PEOPLE........61
   The Four P's...66
TIPS AND TRICKS FOR PRESENTING 83

CHAPTER ONE

TRAINING DOESN'T NEED TO BE BORING

How many times have you sat through a presentation and said to the person next to you, 'when is this ever going to end? This is so boring'. The trainer appears to be just going through the numbers and ticking the boxes.

Or even worse, have you ever really wanted to learn something, yet you feel the trainer just isn't explaining it for you.

So how do you deliver high impact training? Training that is highly effective and highly enjoyable both for the audience and the Trainer. Training so good that when you get it right, the audience have a much higher retention and understanding of the material that you're teaching. Where the audience have a lot more fun because it's a much better learning environment and it creates positive, lasting change in the people that you're training. It's a nice idea, right?

This type of training is actually quite simple. But not easy. It takes a different perspective to create high impact training.

In order to do this, what we need to focus on is three primary areas.

The first area that you've got to focus on is your audience, and how to engage them in a completely new and different way to what most trainers and presenters have learnt.

The second area you've got to focus on is how to create an inspiring learning environment.

And the third area is to be able to self-assess your presenting, give and receive feedback about the way you're doing things so that you can adapt it to your audience.

When you really engage well with your audience and you create an inspiring learning environment, and you become self-aware as a presenter, what you'll find is, this is the place where you really create much better retention and understanding.

When done well this results in a higher learning retention, a much more enjoyable learning environment and a highly effective change for your attendees.

This is where we create lasting positive change in your audience members and for the organisations that you're working so hard for.

To help you understand how this is done, the process is broken down into three areas.

1. Understanding our audience
2. Creating a positive learning environment.
3. Developing ourselves as presenters through feedback.

CHAPTER TWO

NEVER LEAVE A SOLDIER BEHIND

Some years ago, I was responsible for recruit training in one of the armed forces. A part of the training was weapons training. It was delivered as 'dry drills training'. The recruits have the weapons, but they don't have rounds (bullets). So, the weapon and the magazine (ammunition holder) are empty. This was obviously going to be the safest way of introducing weapons training.

During one of these training sessions a weapons trainer came to my office and informed me that they were about to fail and remove from training one of the recruits. (let's call him Jonesy)

"Why are you failing Jonesy? What's wrong with Jonesy?"

"He just doesn't get it, we've done it over and over again, and Jonesy's not getting it, so we want to fail him and remove him from training, he's just not cut out for this"

I said "okay, send Jonesy to me."

I took Jonesy to one side, and we went through the weapons training together.

Now if you've never been involved with weapons training in the military, it's done in a very loud voice, and it's said very, very quickly, in a tone that's a bit aggressive and a little intense. It doesn't give you a lot of time to think.

Just to help you get the picture, you've got rounds (bullets) that are inside the magazine, (this is the bit that movie stars drops off and replaces when he/she runs out of ammunition) and you have the chamber which is the start of the barrel, where rounds enter the weapon. So, the instructor will shout out the drill such as "Weapon firing, weapon stops"(students should now cock the weapon to see what the problem is) "On looking inside you will see rounds in the magazine, no rounds in the chamber" (That means you have to let the working part go forward to load a round into the chamber and continue firing) The drill instructor delivers many orders in this fashion, one of them being "weapon firing , weapon stops, on looking inside you will see, rounds in the magazine and a round lodged in the chamber".

For that the troop is supposed to think, 'hang on, round lodged in the chamber, rounds in the magazine, I'm supposed to put my safety catch on, take my magazine off, tilt the weapon over, shake out that round. Put the magazine back on, let the working parts go forward and continue firing.' That's the natural thing to do if you know what's going on.

Anyway, this is the part Jonesy couldn't get, so I removed him from the stressful environment and the shouting instructor, and said, 'okay let's go through this slowly'.

I teamed up with another instructor to slowly talk him through it, whilst I observed "okay, weapon is firing, rounds are going out of the weapon. Then weapon stops firing, you cock the handle and you look inside. On looking inside, you can see there are rounds in the magazine and there's a round lodged in the chamber." That's when Jonesy said to us, "but there isn't. There isn't a round in the magazine, and there are no rounds in the chamber, I can't see them. Every time he shouts that out, I look inside, but I can't see the rounds, they're not there and I don't know what to do."

It was obvious to me that we needed to show Jonesy this task in a different way so we got an inert round, one that was not going to cause any problems and pushed it into the chamber and placed one in the top of the magazine to show him that's what the instructor meant, there's a round now lodged in the chamber and there are rounds in the magazine, what would you do? He goes, "Oh that's easy, I put my safety catch on, I take my magazine off, I tilt the weapon over and shake the round out and then I put the magazine back on, let the working parts go forward, take off my safety catch and continue firing." …. Perfect Jonesy…well done.

Something was made very simple for that young man on that day, because of that we kept a trainee, we kept somebody in the force. So, somebody could be educated and move forward.

CHAPTER THREE

ACCELERATED LEARNING

This type of training is called accelerated learning, changing things for some people, because not everything's that simple. Sometimes people may think they're a really good trainer but are they really? What's the message that's actually coming across?

The lesson that comes out of that is that there isn't just one way to train people.

The training regime was sound the system had worked for many, step one do this, step two do that, but now we had Jonesy who was the exception to the rules and found it difficult to imagine there being a round in the chamber, and his brain just didn't compute that. If you go with the traditional way, he's a fail, he just couldn't do it. What I did was to say we don't want to lose someone just because our training doesn't necessarily fit with his or her way of understanding the information. A minor tweak in the training has meant the world of difference to that learner.

Some trainers think it's more important that the trainer themselves need to know the information and have a loud and fast confident delivery.

It may be the way they were trained, the old adage of "if they don't understand …shout louder." However, a better training environment would be to think are my students getting this or am I going too fast. There is a danger the student may be left behind and not fully understand what's going on.

I have seen this often when people deliver Power Point presentations, step one, step two, step three, step four and so on. They read their way through it and they look at the audience, and they think oh, I'll just move on to step five. Now there could be that person who doesn't understand the magazine and the rounds in the chamber type scenario in the lesson, but they just move on because it's time to move on. So, if you don't fully understand what's in front of you and where your audience are, and you continue with your lesson then they're lost. This results with a learner who's lost and slipping through the cracks.

For example, if that's important information, perhaps emergency procedures or in situations where the consequences of getting it wrong are quite significant, then by not making sure everyone has understood, you are potentially leaving a very weak link in the chain.

The trainer needs to understand the students' level of knowledge first. "First seek to understand before being understood" As Steven Covey put it.

A lot of people want to pass the exam, or get the certificate, and that's their end goal. But as a trainer your end goal should be, they shouldn't be leaving without understanding the information. The certificates are nice to have, but it's the information's which is a need to have, quite often that's done the other way around.

The trainers' responsibility is to adapt the way they deliver training to make certain that people don't just get the certificate but truly understand the information along the way.

We could have a Jonesy that gets tripped up on one part of the process. It's important as trainers that we don't lose people along the way because we failed to understand their needs.

It's o.k. to say I don't understand

If you were the Jonesy in the story, then you'd probably be thinking 'Thank goodness Sarge took a moment to explain that to me in a different way.' It was a light bulb moment for that young man, it was like 'oh this is what it is,' and very quickly he was straight back into training and carried on and passed the course.

You've got to create an environment where it's okay to say, excuse me but I don't get this, encouraging them to put their hand up and say, I don't get this, please help me.

CHAPTER FOUR

FINDING A MORE EFFECTIVE WAY

Another way

There's always a different way. There are a lot of people going to a lesson or a class and they say this is what I always do when I deliver this lesson. It's the same every time, but it shouldn't be. Try this, today....

I'm going to deliver the information however these people in front of me require it to be delivered. Get their engagement, get their buy-in, create rapport, this is what we need to do. It's the same information but it's just unloaded differently.

Creating a good environment for learning

We can find their needs by questioning people on where they are in the class when they arrive. Such as …

1. Tell me a little bit about yourself?
2. How long have you been doing this?
3. What do you expect to get out of this lesson?
4. Where is your level of knowledge in this area?

Make it nice and comfortable, where it's okay not to know anything, and it's also okay to be the specialist. If you open the room up early, it helps you deliver your information better.

If you've got those people who are super switched on in the class, you can refer to them and it brings them on too. Even if they didn't want to be there because they think they already know it', by utilizing that person in the environment, "Well John's a specialist here, John what is your take on this?" John's like, "Oh yes, I can talk about that for a moment." We get his knowledge and the person who doesn't know gets to learn it, and it's a nice comfortable training environment.

It's not all about the trainer; it's about the trainer facilitating the entire learning environment so that everyone wins. The trainer is facilitating the class, the learning, and the knowledge. You have your message that you've got to get across, but it won't go across if you don't facilitate it properly.

That's a significant difference between the old version of training and the new training that is required for today's work environment culture.

I've seen a lot of trainers that go into a session and they say, "okay we all know this is a boring subject, we'll get through this as quickly as we can, it's uncomfortable I know but we'll have to do what we can. Please leave all questions till the end, and I'll start now. One, two, three, four, five."

You don't know who's in your room. There could be somebody thinking, I've got to go soon to pick up my children. Or somebody may have turned up at the last minute, rushed in to sign on the attendance sheet and is now bursting for the toilet, and is going to think about that for the next 10 to 15 minutes and not listen to anything you say.

Developing my style.

I joined the military straight from school and I thoroughly enjoyed the camaraderie and engagement with other people.

I was always engaged with people. When I got promoted to Corporal, I had other people I was responsible for, and I thoroughly enjoyed teaching them and watching their development. This led me into putting my hand up for an instructional role and my thoughts moving to "wow this is really interesting, I'm really enjoying this".

Back in the days of OHPs, (overhead projectors) clear plastic sheets had information printed on them and you stuck them on a screen. Well I didn't like words on a screen, so I got some clear sheets and drew my own pictures on them. Obviously, I was going to speak the words myself and I didn't want people reading them whilst I was talking to them. Reading is an adult activity that's best done alone...... unless you are in a book club it's not something, we all do together.

People used to find that interesting. 'This guy's interesting he's got some funny pictures and he knows what he's talking about.' It could've been a cartoon picture of an airplane with some bits falling off, or a burst tyre, or a scene of something happening to somebody. It was just a visual aid, it put a picture to my words.

I found the traditional way that you were taught to train was a little bit dry and you could actually get a better result by innovating a few small things in the actual training, like drawings rather than just text, or getting up out of the classroom, going for a walk around. "Let's go and have a look at one of these in real life." Just trying to do anything to stop the student sitting down on his bum facing forward and watching the instructor read.

I found that using visual aids, engaging with my students, changing the environment and having fun was getting really good results.

All my lesson preps and my hand outs were drawings or mind maps, they were very different from my peers, but I was having fun and the students were engaged.

That continued for a good six years in an engineering environment, moving around, getting accelerated, doing lots of different and interesting things with learning styles.

When I went on my next promotion course for the next rank. I experienced the then new "Experiential Learning and Authentic Leadership".

I thought, "wow this is fantastic", it's all about your brain and how we learn best. How we engage with others, and there were lots of accelerated learning techniques on the course and suddenly my light went on and I thought… wow, this is what I've been doing all along and I really want to learn more.

I was successful in gaining a position at the Leadership Development school and it was a fantastic learning environment. High ropes courses, low ropes courses, alternative instructional techniques, high level facilitation, emotional intelligence, counselling, coaching transactional analysis, all the really interesting stuff.

I was like a sponge just soaking it all up, thinking this is educating me on the stuff I've been doing, because I really didn't know that what I'd been doing had a name, but I had been engaging people and inspiring them through accelerated learning techniques, which I thought was normal.

When I eventually left the RAF after 23 years I emigrated to New Zealand with my wife and two children. We packed all our belongings into four bags, our mantra was 'New Job, New Life, New Zealand'.

We bought a one-way ticket and went, "let's go!" in New Zealand I worked for myself for a while with kids who wouldn't stay in school, Alternative Cooperative Education (ACE) kids, they called them.

On my first day I encouraged them to write all their aspirations down on large sheets of paper using large maker pens (graffiti tools) The lady who employed me said "how did you get them to write?" Well I didn't do it by standing there and writing on a board and telling them to write what I did. I got it through engaging them and asking them about what they liked, and eventually moving it around to where we needed to be. Even at their young age there needed to be a respect for the learners in the room.

By spending the time at the beginning of the lesson to find out what they wanted, I was able to dove tail the learning to suit their needs.

I also got work with a company called Training Solutions at Aoraki Polytech, doing induction training for the Fonterra Cheeses Factory and some team building in various organizations.

After a year I moved on again and joined the RNZAF back into the Air Force environment.

I joined the Royal New Zealand Air Force as a technical instructor, back into the technical learning environment and started to accelerate my training at every opportunity.

I taught aerodynamics through the use of a boomerang. I made two boomerangs, one with aerodynamic shapes on it and one just rounded off, so it wouldn't fly.

I knocked on the door of the classroom in the morning and said, "Hey guys come on let's go and throw boomerangs." "Ok but aren't we supposed to be doing aerodynamics"? they responded.

"Forget that, I've made these, let's go and have some fun." We ran out to the airfield with two boomerangs. I threw mine and it came back.

They threw theirs and it landed on the grass near the runway. I said, you better go and get that because that's where the aircraft land. So, they ran off and retrieved it. I took it off them and said, you're not very good with that, give it to somebody else. I threw mine again, it came back, they threw theirs and it landed on the grass again. So, they brought it back, after two or three goes they wanted to throw mine. I said, okay you can throw mine, but first I'm going to throw yours because I think you're not throwing it right. So, I threw theirs and it landed on the grass again.

They threw mine and it came back, and then they looked at mine and compared it to theirs, and they said, they're different. I said, "No, they're not, they are both the same shape."

They said, "No, they're not, they're different." They looked and found that the leading edge on mine was slightly different to theirs. The trailing edge was more pointed, theirs was squarer. So yes, they were different I had filed the leading and trailing edges on mine to the same cross section as a wing. Theirs was the same shape but the leading and training edges were square so it would not fly.

Out there on the grass through throwing the boomerang and watching it go up, and always fly to the left no matter which way it was thrown, we worked out lift, weight, thrust and drag and talked about it in an accelerated learning environment.

When we came back to the classroom and flashed on the presentation, most of the information had been experienced and we were just touching off on a few points. The lesson flowed well.

It was a fairly unique experience for a group of military guys and girls, who were thinking they were going to get the traditional 'here's all the information up on an overhead Power Point' To now going outside and actually doing experiential learning, but the effect was profound on them. It did in fact accelerate their learning quite dramatically.

On another occasion I walked into the classroom with a whole box full of nuts and bolts. I was supposed to teach them about the different nuts and bolts, and how there are hundreds of different fasteners on an aircraft.

As I walked through the classroom door I purposefully tripped and threw the whole lot across the floor. I went "Oh my God, sorry guys, we better get these picked up." They started picking them up, saying, "what's this? This is a funny thing." I said, "I don't know, what do we think that could be for?" We engaged everybody to think what it could be used for and where would we find that on the aircraft? Let's go and have a look and if we can find one of these on a real aircraft. That kind of thing, yes, it was fun, some people thought it was different, but I addressed every fastener, every reason why and where it would be used. It just wasn't on a Power Point. It was done through interaction, through setting the room and more importantly involving the people in their learning.

It did move them on quickly, other trainers started taking an interest in my lessons and delivery style. The Senior Trainer who was in charge of me at the time, said, "Brian you're not only training the students, you're training the staff too!"

Other trainers started trying different teaching techniques for themselves and were getting positive results. Training had become fun and engaging and the results were showing, the students were learning quicker and there were less failures.

It got to the point where somebody would come to me and say, "Brian I've got two people who are failing, have you got any ideas how we can help them?" And

I'd say, "Yeah there's lots we can do to support them." It wasn't what had traditionally been done but it was working!

For instance, two guys had failed an exam, the Senior Trainer asked, can you do something to help them? Traditionally they would re-read the notes and try again to pass the exam.

This wasn't going to do it. So, I said, "okay sit back to back, we're going to play a game. You're going to start off John telling me everything you know about aerodynamics", or whatever the subject was that they'd failed, hydraulics, engineering, pneumatics etc. "Tell me everything you know, if you stop talking Steve's going to take over and he's going to tell me everything he knows."

It was like a little competition, they were trying not to stop talking, and it was all coming out. As soon as one stopped talking the other would fire off, and he would say just whatever's inside his head relevant to the subject. I would ask a few searching questions around what had been said and further information would emerge. Both students amazed themselves with the knowledge they actually did have in their heads.

They passed the exam the next day.

It was just a different way of thinking.... How do people learn and understand what they need to know? All of those experiences, (and many more) both in the military and in the civilian world, dealing with teenagers, dealing with adults, has really led me to rethink the way training could be done. In fact, it's helped me to reposition the way to accelerate learning for trainers into this new model I've developed.

The Present your best model

The model looks at the three areas to develop.
1. You've got to create buy-in.
2. It's got to be a healthy interactive Adult Learning Environment.
3. There must be an element of fun and Experiential Activity.

We have V1.0 (the old version) where buy-in was expected, the environment was somewhat boring and playing games was deemed to be for children only.

And now we have V2.0 (the new version) where buy-in is created, the environment is interactive and engaging, and games and activities are encouraged to promote experiential learning.

The Model

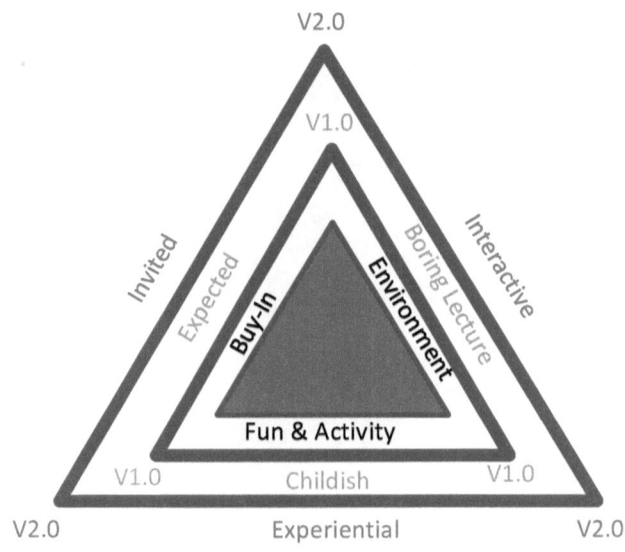

CHAPTER FIVE

UNWRAPPING THE MODEL

The triangle represents the three critical elements to training people and accelerating their learning.

The three elements are:-

1. You've got to create buy-in.

People have got to want to be there. Sometimes people are thrust into an environment because that's the process in their learning, but if you can make them want to be there, create the buy-in so they enjoy the experience, that's a much better place to start the learning. process.

They need to know what's in it for me? Why am I here? What am I going to get from this? How's it going to go? Am I going to enjoy it? Will I be able to nip out and get a coffee, or have a drink of water? Doodle on my desk, or whatever it requires. (The doodle on the desk thing, I used to stick paper on the desk of the students I was teaching and say to people, just go mad, if you want to draw something, draw on there). When they went to lunch, I'd often have a look at what doodles had been created and there'd be some amazing things drawn on there. Some were lesson orientated doodles some were just abstract. It's incredible how allowing that freedom to doodle away was creating the buy-in for some people.

2. A Healthy Adult Learning Environment.

The second part is to remember that you're trying to create a healthy adult learning environment. One where it's okay to get up and go to the toilet without getting permission. Or to ask a question right now while its fresh in your mind, knowing if you don't ask it now then you never will. Or if you don't quite understand this bit, it's okay to say that in this environment?

Knowing for sure that you're not going to get put down, or have to wear the dunce hat, will give your students the confidence to explore and learn, because you are acknowledging that we all learn differently?

The adult learning environment is different to the environment that many of us experienced in school. Where it was not okay to ask questions, or you felt like you had to fit into a box.

When creating an adult learning environment, I always say to people, when I'm teaching it's okay for you to do anything that may help your learning in this class. If you want to get up and walk around, do so. If you want to doodle all over your book (it's theirs) do so. If you need to take a break, speak up and we'll break sooner rather than later. It doesn't take long before things settle into a workable rhythm.

The way training used to be was sit down, face the front, say nothing and don't move, which was terrible for learning. Once my son who was very inquisitive, wanted to ask a question, he put his hand up and waited (as he had been taught) but the teacher's response was. "Not now, get back in your hole." That teacher may have felt in control but what was happening to the child's learning ability for the rest of the lesson?

3. There must be an element of fun and activity.

A happy brain learns faster, scientist have told us the best three things to fire up the endorphins in our brains are: - 3rd Movement, 2nd Laughter and 1st Singing.

You should allow people the ability to move, the human body thrives on **movement** (no one likes sitting still in a classroom for hours on end) It's okay if someone wants to get up and walk to the window and then walk back and sit down. Where as a child in school you would get told off for that, what are you doing? sit still, face the front and listen.

Laughter helps you learn

Then you've got **laughter**, your brain is really lit up when you're laughing. You can always remember when you last had a good laugh and what was going on, because your brain was lit up. Get some humour into your lessons. Find the fun in your subject and magnify it.

When you are **singing**, your brain is really on fire. If you can get singing into your lesson then you're a genius trainer, BUT and it's a big but, they have to want to sing.

I once had a group of students that I was teaching the subject of Managing Diversity, recognising and valuing the different, skills and abilities that we all bring to the party.

I split my group of 24 into three teams of eight. The first group I told to practice a special skill, stamping their right foot. Whilst they did that, I told the second group to practice their special skill of stamping their left foot. The third groups special skill was to clap.

Each team had a few minutes to practice their skills and ensure their team could produce the sound at the same time. I then briefed the three teams that the first group would demonstrate their sound only once, followed by group two, then group three, then keep on repeating the process.

The result was STAMP, STAMP, CLAP, STAMP, STAMP, CLAP over and over. After several rounds it starts to sound really good and I burst into song

"Buddy *you're a boy you're a big boy playing in the street gonna be a big man someday, you've got mud on your face, you big disgrace kicking your can all over the place....*

Then I just stopped singing and every time I have done this (many times) the groups have all sang in unison….. *We will, We will, Rock you, Rock you…..(sounds great)* But here's the point…no one told them to sing they did it because they wanted to and whenever I bumped into any of those past students they always talked about the fantastic Managing Diversity lesson they enjoyed so much.

Throw out the old rule book

There is a fear for some people, 'Oh this is not structured, this is not as it should be' but it's learning, it's fun and it works. As a trainer you already have the knowledge, you just have to be brave enough to give it a try.

The result of that new way of training is extremely effective and will quite literally shorten the time span for learning.

It's an accelerated learning process, when people meet something like that again they will think, "Oh I remember when I learnt that it was fun and engaging". Those students with the boomerangs, I can imagine, that every time they see a boomerang, they will remember this is how they learnt theory of flight, let me tell you about it. That's because it's was a strong memory and they can easily retrieve it. It's something to relate to rather than trying to remember a sheet of paper with some words on.

Creating an Adult learning environment

The three elements that create an adult learning environment are

1. An environment where they can ask questions.

2. An environment where movement is okay.

3. An environment where we can have some fun and activity.

Particularly laughter and music. Some people think games are childish, but they allow that inner child to come out and to learn. People learn really well through games and activities.

A lot of people learn through touching, doing, exploring. If you can put something in there that's going to challenge their brain, and you're going to stand back, shut up and let them get on with it, then it's so much better. It's where a lot of leadership team building activities take place, you set them a task to problem solve, they go off and they learn through that, and then you debrief the learning points afterwards.

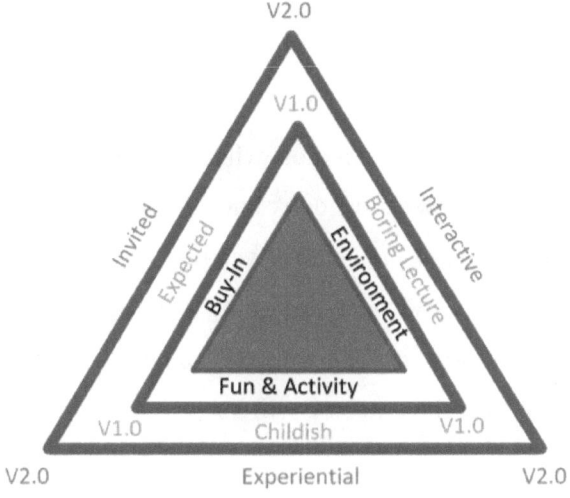

If we go back to our triangle and look at the fun and activity. It was deemed to be childish for adults to play games, "I can't do that, I've got a shirt and a tie, I'm a CEO, how can I possibly play a game? My people won't respect me." But if you take that tie off, and actually roll your sleeves up and get involved in the activity, your people will respect you and you'll learn a lot more of what's going on.

As the famous German playwright Bertolt Brecht once said "if you don't have fun you don't have a show". If you don't have some fun and explore these things, how will you know?

Quite often we learn most when we are brave enough to just show what we don't know. With games a lot of people don't like to get involved because they don't like to look silly. Why are they going to look silly? Because they are not familiar with the activity or they don't know what the outcome will be.

If they are not familiar with something and they don't know what the outcomes going to be, what's going to happen? They are going to learn something.

The old version, the version 1.0 does not include activities. With version 2.0 you allow for activities to be creative, interesting, and engaging.

For instance, when I was teaching Adair's Functional Approach to Leadership, part of the lesson was…What are the needs of the three areas? (the team, the task, the individual). A Simple activity I created for that was, I got three large sheets of paper. I printed the words Team needs on one, Task needs on the second and Individual needs on the 3rd. I then stuck them on three tables at areas around the outside of the building we were training in. They were about 150 meters apart. I split the group into three teams and sent them off on a mission. To go out find the tables and write on the sheets all the things that they thought fitted that sheet. For instance, the needs of the task, such as timings, the costings, the effectiveness, the resources etc.

When they had spent five minutes on a task they had to go and find the next one and continue to rotate around the three tables. Each time coming across what the other teams had put on the sheet. So now they had to add something to what was already written, (if they could think of anymore). The last team at teach table would retrieve the sheet and bring it back to the classroom and we'd pin it up and discuss their comments.

So, we've got people moving around, it's a very simple activity. They've been involved, their brains are fired up. They've written some information down, the learning was so much easier than sitting down saying, right what are the needs? Just allowing that movement to take place, and while they're off in their little groups they can ask the questions that they may not feel like they can ask you in the classroom, because they might feel a bit silly. The more creative and engaging you can make activities in version 2.0, the more your students are going to remember and easily recall their learning.

Put an action to learning and it ties the whole thing together. We can remember things that we did far better than the things that we read. Putting actions to learning assist greatly, obviously you can't do it with every single thing, but if you just stop and think, could I do something here in the classroom?

Even just getting outside for a discussion in the fresh air and then coming back in. For those who find it difficult to try new things then follow the words of Yoda, "there is no try only do" or as Nike so plainly put it "Just do it". It works and your students will love you for it.

Buy-in

Now let's talk about creating the buy-in. Buy-in was generally expected. You're on this course what do you expect, you're supposed to be here for an hour and a half, and we're talking hieroglyphics, or whatever they're talking about. You're expected to want to sit there, face the front and be interested because you're on the course.

In a lot of corporate environments, or a lot of commercial environments, you've got people who really don't want to be there, so that old model of you're here, you must be attentive doesn't really work for everybody.

It's quite frustrating that it's still the case even today; people go to a lot of courses that they don't enjoy, they don't want to be there. They were sent there because somebody higher up couldn't make it, but the company had to send someone.

Or it's a safety training course where you're a fire warden or emergency warden, and it's your secondary role and you have to do it, and you don't really want to be there. I've been involved in training some of those courses, and there are some grumpy people who do not want to be there. I had a gentleman say to me once, 'how long is this shit going to take?' (I was like, oh that's nice isn't it). I said, 'well what shit are we talking about? Are we talking about the shit where we save people's lives during an emergency'? He immediately apologised and admitted he didn't really want to be here. I gave my usual 100% to the training, created buy in, respected the room, had some fun and activity and plenty of audience engagement.

After the session the same chap came over shook my hand and said "Hey that was brilliant thank you so much, sorry for my initial comments but it's just been so dull in the past and I just wasn't looking forward to it".

So, as we can see poor training techniques can have a detrimental effect, it can add to peoples already negative assumptions about the training.

Also other students who were perhaps considering how they were going to approach training may be affected in a negative way. All because a loud person is making an objection. It can have a detrimental effect and as a trainer it can affect you too. 'Oh my God they don't want to be here', and you'll find yourself talking quickly, rushing through your information. You look at your watch and suddenly realise it's all finished yet you have only been going a short while.

I had a young man once teaching breathing apparatus (BA), which was at least an hour's lesson. The students were all older men and he was quite a young guy.

He looked nervous and didn't create any buy-in at all, he just stood up and said, "Right guys this is pretty painful, I know you've all done it before so we'll get through it as quick as we can." He got through it in 10 minutes. I was observing at the time, but 10 minutes and he was all done.

Those people didn't know how to operate a BA; they were the ones who were going to have to use it. So we had to slow it down, redo the lesson, find out where people were using questions like…. Who has used this before? One person said "I have, but I've only used it once and that was five years ago". Another said "I use it all the time every day, I'm just here for a refresher". Hey how about you two work together and help each other.

Asking open questions such as when have you used it? What have you done? How many times? We create that environment; we create the buy-in so that people want to be there. It's particularly crucial in training that involves safety, because if any of these people don't know how to correctly use the breathing apparatus then their lives could potentially be in danger.

You'll be amazed at how many students will just bluff their way through things and hope they learn it back in the workplace, which is the wrong place to learn it. Yes, you gain your experience in the workplace, but fundamental basics are learnt on the course.
We invite people in, ask them questions, ask them what they are thinking and what they want to get from the training session.

Focusing on the buy-in of your students, even before you start any of the official training, is a really vital part of creating a positive learning environment, rather than just assuming they're engaged.

Fun and Activity

A very simple way to invite people in and is also a nice little ice breaker, is just give them all a post-it note and say, just write three things on there that you want to get from this lesson.

It could be anything you like at all. The grumpy guy might write, I want to go home early, or something silly like that. Others may write learn a bit more about BA or whatever it is.

When they've all got their three you give them a minute or so, and say, "Okay so you've got three things each, now turn to the person next to you, together you've got six things now let's end up with three.

So, they sit together, and the bloke who's put, I want to go home early, suddenly feels a bit like well that's not a good one is it really? So that one goes out the window. Between them they come up with three fairly good ones. I say, "Okay now each group of two has got three between them, now work with another group of two. We've now got four people, looking at six things, lets end up with three. More rubbish ones go out the window and more positive discussions take place. Eventually we end up with the whole group refining the last 6 and we end up with one sheet of paper with the three agreed outcomes of the lesson.

I take those and write them on the board. They are generally in the realms of what we are going to teach, and everybody has been a part of putting that on the board.

I would then say to people, "Okay so we've all been involved in creating this, are these the three things that we must walk away with, if nothing else from this course, is there anything else that we need to put on the board now before we start?

One of them always turns out to be fun, which is nice. Somebody always asks for fun, so we leave it on there, and yeah, we all want to have some fun, we want to enjoy what we're doing. We want to walk away having enjoyed the training and gained valuable information on the subjects, this creating buy in has always worked well for me. Everybody's happy to start because they've been involved, they feel valued, they are ready, let's go.

Environment

Next we're talking about the healthy adult learning environment side, an environment where it is okay to ask all and any questions. It is okay to come in and then go back out. It is okay to answer your phone if you need to answer your phone.

We've all got children and families, and external diversions. There could be some things that you do need to answer your phone for. If you say to everybody, make sure your cell phones are turned to silent; I don't want you interrupting the class today. Somebody's thinking, well I need mine on. You could rephrase that to, okay guys, I'm going to turn my cell phone to silent because I don't want to be disturbed whilst I'm teaching this lesson. Now if you need yours on by all means have it on, but please ensure its on silent and if you do take a call just leave the class, it's not a problem because real life happens. People think, 'ah that's okay, I don't need to worry about that now, I can focus on what I'm going to do. In fact, I'm just going to turn mine off anyway.

Whereas if they're worrying about, I need my phone on but it might ring, I better turn it down, (all this will be going on.) People can get stressed inside their head, which takes away from the learning. Even down to some people have to stick things in their face and set fire to them (smoking) and they have to do that every

15 or 20 minutes or they get grumpy, or they stop listening, or they continue to think about that.

Thinking when's he going to shut up because I want to go for a smoke. Address this at the start, ask them, hey, does anybody smoke in the class? Yeah, well I tell you what we'll take a short break round about 20 minutes and you can nip outside for five minutes, the rest of us will have a comfort break. Then people are aware of what's going to happen.

It used to be students didn't know what was going to happen because they were under the control of the instructor, and you did as he or she told you to. When you create a healthy adult learning environment, you're facilitating learning.

The difference between the old way and the new way is as different as night and day. Particularly when it comes to the results and the ability of your students to actually absorb that information, integrate that information into their workday, and then actually recall it when it's necessary.

CHAPTER SIX

3 FRUSTRATIONS OF TRAINING PEOPLE

| 1. Understanding our audience |
| 2. Creating a positive learning environment. |
| 3. Developing ourselves as presenters through feedback. |

In any learning environment there are two separate entities if you like. You've got the trainer, who will have their concerns and frustrations, and hopes and goals, and you've got the students/audience.

We've talked a little bit about the three pillars of the model: -

1. looking at your audience.
2. looking at creating an inspiring learning environment.
3. The presenter, actually being fairly engaging.

Let's talk about each one of those and the kinds of frustrations that you're seeing happen out in the workplace when we're training.

<u>Frustration One</u>

Engaging the audience

Where are the frustrations that we are seeing in engaging with the audience?

If you don't engage the audience, they don't connect with you, there's no rapport. There's no joy, there's no enjoyment in the lesson, there's no fun. There's just… this is the road we're going down.

If you don't engage with people, it creates an 'I don't want to be here' attitude, which then becomes 'I'm going to be a bit awkward and I'm going to ask you some tricky questions, because you're annoying me, you haven't respected me, or engaged with me at all. You don't even know why I'm here, where I'm from, what my knowledge is and so I'm going to ask you the tricky questions because I want to trip you up.'

You've actually got somebody who could possibly start not a fight with you, but a mental game.

The trainers who are reading this will say, yup I've had that guy. He knows the answer, he's been here 20 years, but what he's saying is, "why didn't you tell everybody that I've been here for 20 years? Why am I now having to say things that lets everybody know that I know the stuff that you're talking about?"

You caused that because you didn't engage with them. You've potentially got the guys and girls who are disengaged and more than disengaged they actually try to disrupt the entire process by drawing attention to themselves. This has an effect on both the learners and the trainer.

An effect on the trainer would be to feel a bit uncomfortable, "I don't like this, why's this person doing this?" You might find yourself placating that person and delivering the training to that person, rather than where it needs to go to the rest of the class. So you're focused on that problem, that little itch on your side. You have to keep scratching it, because you haven't gone there. If you're a student sitting in the audience and the trainer hasn't engaged you, then there's an element of frustration about that as well.

They will sense that the trainer isn't very good at their job. They can't handle a tricky person in the room. They'll recognize that there's this awful person making noise, but they'll think well he's not doing a very good job. They'll either feel sorry for you or they may even join the fight.

All this is going on and it's taking away from the learning, because there's something else happening. you're now dealing with the situation, rather than dealing with what you're trying to present. It's a distraction.

When we get this wrong, when we get buy-in wrong and when you see trainers who don't take the time to engage their audience well, we can see the detrimental effects are quite profound. Detrimental effects on learning. Detrimental effects on the students not enjoying their environment, and the trainer not enjoying delivering the training.

However, when you get it right it's fantastic. A trainer knows when he's got it right, because he's built rapport, the lesson went well, the flow was good. People come on board, those people who are knowledgeable offer suggestions rather than tricky questions. You can ask them, hey John what do you think of this? He'll put a nice point across and help you cover off something that you might have been a bit vague with.

They influence others in a positive way in the classroom. The flow has now become nice, it's back and forward, and it's a relaxed learning environment, where people don't need to worry about the fight between the instructor and the stroppy guy.

They start to think this is really good, I'm enjoying this, I'm getting information from lots of different avenues, but it's all relevant. The trainer is facilitating through engagement with the students and learning is taking place.

The Four P's

When you get this pillar right, of engaging your audience it's a fantastic environment for both the trainer and the audience, and the learning outcome is positive and memorable for all.

There's a tool I use for engaging my audience it's called the four P's. (Prisoner, Protester, Passenger and Participant)

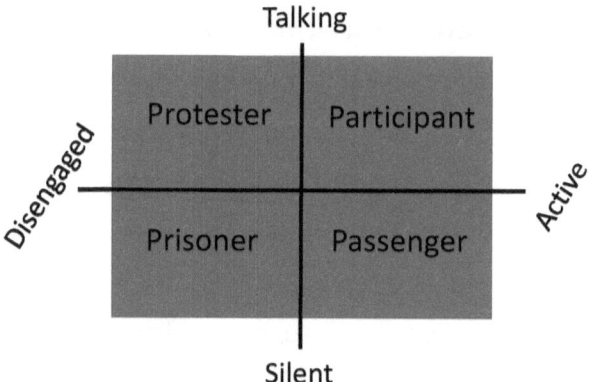

When I start a class. I say to people, 'Hi my names Brian, how are we doing today team? Where are you from? What do you do?' A little bit of that ground level communication chat and then I will say, I just want to show you something that I found 20 odd years ago, it's getting a bit old but it's still relevant today. It's the four windows we view our lives through. No matter what we're doing we're always looking through one of these windows. Sometimes I'll say, "Okay imagine at Christmas time your off work and you're getting paid, oh I'll have some of that thank you very much, I'm a **Participant,** yeah it's all fun and games.

You come back to work after Christmas and you don't really like your job, and you're like oh God, is this what I really do? But you don't tell anybody that, you're just thinking "I'm a bit of a **Prisoner** in this work place".

Then somebody gives you a task that you don't like, and you tell them, why do I have to do that, I don't like it, It's not my turn etc.? Now you're a **Protestor**.

Some days you go to work you go through the motions you go home, you take nothing from the day, you add nothing of value you are just a **Passenger** on the bus of life going wherever the bus goes.

Now when I show that to a class I'll just go through the windows and say, I'm not putting you in a box. I'm just letting you know that I know that we all live our lives through these windows, you may be experiencing any one of these, but you can choose any one you want.

So if you are sitting there today, because somebody sent you and told you, you are to do this course, I'm feeling for you because I wouldn't like that to happen to me.

But you know, you can get some benefit from this, it's over to you, but I certainly feel that same frustration that you do.

Then I say sometimes people come on course and say "how longs this going to take I've got things to do? They are Protesting, they're having a go at me, they're going to spend the next 45 minutes protesting, they're not really going to get the best from today, they don't want to be here and they want to let me and everybody else know. Amazingly this always gets a laugh, normally from the person who was going to be the protester but has now realised it's not a good place to be.

Then we've got the passenger, people who may turn up, they're kind of okay with it, but they're not going to offer any advice. They're not going to get involved, they're just along for the ride. They normally spend time checking their phone or using their laptop to do business whilst they are here. Trying to multi-task but really not focusing on either subject fully so may miss something vital. At this point people tend to put their phones and laptops away.

The window that we all should be in is the participant window. Because this information here today is for you, to help you, so the more you get involved, the more questions you ask, the better it's going to be and the more you will take away.

By showing people that simple model of the four P's it acknowledges their feelings, grievances etc and if they were going to protest they kind of shake that off and think, oh yes, that was going to be me, he gets it, I don't have to act it up, because he gets it already.
It's delivered in a nice way, not all right, this is where you are, this is what I'm telling you. But hey guys, I'm

aware that any time in our lives we could be anywhere on this picture.

You just appreciate where people are, not everybody in front of you wants to be there, and some are told to be there. Particularly if you're delivering something like an emergency warden training session.

Just acknowledging the state of mind that each of the participants may be in, is an extremely great tool to engage them where they're at and create connection and rapport between the trainer and the participant.
 I've often had people say to me after I've shared this, well actually I was going to be a protester but I feel all right now (a little laugh) I think I'm moving across towards that passenger bit.

 They tell me where they are and later on if it's a whole day session, or a longer training session, you'll hear people use the terms between themselves. I was a right protester when I got here but I'm not now. Or I was a bit of a prisoner this morning, I didn't want to come but I'm really enjoying this. You can hear them use those words themselves to describe what they were or where they were at.

Frustration Two

The Environment

You've heard the term "**Death by Power Point**," and that's what most people think they're walking into. Particularly if you've got a Power Point set up and that's all you've got set up and the rooms darkened and everything's facing the front. They go, here we go. They're already going home before they get in the classroom.

Simple things like just having a white board with a hand crafted welcome or a flip chart with a cartoon intro on it.

When I was teaching fire safety training, I used to draw cartoons of the lesson road map and people would often come and take a picture of my board. I'd ask why are you taking pictures and they would say " I want to show my friends what we learnt" and "I like your pictures they are cool"? It's just a little cartoon, so every time they see the cartoon, they are reminded of the training. They've been inspired to remember things. It's easier for them to take that information away, they'll retain it for much longer.

Also having a few fun items on the tables or a brief roadmap of the training and having a 10 second chat with people on their way in, makes for a more open and inspiring environment.

If you rely solely on a Power Point presentation it can become dull and boring, and people get distracted, they start fidgeting, they start looking outside. They start talking to their friend, they start looking at their watch. You'll only get their attention if you mention their name, 'Sorry I wasn't really listening, and can you go back again?' This will disrupt your flow; it's just not happening for you. You don't even know what they want from it because you never asked them.
Somebody could even be in the wrong class, 'oh this isn't the environment I'm supposed to be in. I'm supposed to be next door,' and that has happened!

When that happens you always think, am I any good at this? People start to doubt themselves; I'm not enjoying it either. Maybe I could have done better, done something different but this is the way I was shown or this is the way it happened to me so it's going to happen to them.

You need to change the environment into a nice adult environment, make it acceptable, make it a fun place to be, a place where people want to be. If you go somewhere and you're going to show a presentation, and you've closed all the curtains and made it dark, that's not very appealing. If possible, keep the curtains open or the lights on nice and bright until you need to start the presentation. You could even ask for assistance from your students.

Everyone's hoping to be entertained a little bit. We're all entertainers as instructors and presenters so entertain them, involve them , inspire them, enthuse them. Make them want to sit here, point things out to them that are quite nice. "Look where we are today, we're on the 13th floor, what a fantastic view we've got of the city. Were just appreciating where we are today. Nobody's going to be bothering you for the next hour because you've got the time booked out, you don't really have to work, that's my job.

Help yourself to the tea and the coffee, there's some note pads if you want to use them. Just make it really nice". Have a bit of fun, a bit of laughter, allow people to move around. Sit where they like not where you tell them to sit. Quite often people are coming to a class and want to sit at the back. If you say no, come sit at the front. They won't move because they don't feel comfortable or confident and they think that they will get asked all the questions. But if you get into a lesson and things are going well, you could then say, actually could you just come a bit closer team and they will.

They know there's no threat, and then they'll move forward. There's no rush to get everybody to the front of the class, but if you're a good presenter you can have them all at the front of the class within 5 or 10 minutes.

Frustration Three

You, (The Presenter)

The third element, the third pillar of the model, is actually about you the presenter. There are so many presenters out there who are just not aware of what they can do to achieve as a presenter. It's awkward, people know when you're not doing well, and you know from their reaction that you're not doing well too. It becomes that awkwardness of this isn't going very well, I'm not enjoying this. Again, you may start to speed up to get through the horrible experience as quick as you can and get out the classroom.

Sometimes that can have a mental effect and if that topic comes up again you may shy away from it. I've had trainers in the past ask me, Brian could you teach this for me? I said, well you're the same as me, why don't you teach it? Oh, I had a terrible session with it last time, it didn't go well at all.
 So they set up a fear in themselves, am I good enough? Can I do this? They're affecting their own self-worth, and now have anxiety issues.

For the audience in the class they generally sense it too, they know, they'll walk away and say, we didn't get what we paid for. We didn't enjoy that, let's not get that person again. Let's not re-engage them.
I've had a job lately where somebody's said to me, can you do some conflict resolution training for us because

the last people who were the 'supposed professionals', we got nothing from.

It was the same information I would deliver but it was down to delivery, and that's all it's going to be. If you the presenter can deliver it in a way that really sticks with them, then you're going to have an audience that's really highly engaged, they won't be getting distracted, and you're going to be their preferred trainer.

You're building credibility, a respect for yourself and people ask for your services again and again.

The information's always going to be information, what they enjoyed was the experience. They enjoyed you, the way you talked, the way you let them talk, the way you used their stories over the top of your stories. It's all about you being aware of you, am I talking too much? Is it all me, me, me? I had a story that happened to me? I had another story happen to me, and then this happened to me. Or is it, has anybody ever had this happen to them? Yes, would you like to share that? Think about this, are you giving too much? Where do you start when you go into a class, where do you greet people? Are you like, "HELLO I'M THE TRAINER, NICE TO MEET YOU" ….. Are you too full on?

There's a lot of things that you could be doing that can be off putting. You can have a negative effect on the people in front of you without even knowing it.

When you get this particular aspect right, you will not only increase your effectiveness as a trainer, but you will also get an increase in your credibility in the organisation.

Now you're seeing that you can help this information really get transmitted across to your audience in a very effective and engaging way. You will generate repeat business as a trainer.

A lot of companies have trainer feedback forms that have to be filled out. They mainly consist of tick and flick boxes and offer little in the way of constructive feedback. How do you know you're getting it right?

Feedback

There's a very good way to find out and that's to get somebody other than a student or audience to observe you. You don't want them to watch the lesson content, 'because you know what the content is. You need that person to watch **you**.

- What you do with your hands?
- What you do with your head?
- Where do you look?
- The way you move about?
- Do you get too close to people?
- Do you talk too fast?
- Are you shouting?
- How is your tone, pitch and rhythm?

Have them observe you (video is good here) and give you some real constructive feedback. If you're bold enough to listen to that feedback, then you'll develop and grow.

If you don't get somebody in you will never really know. **If you don't know, you don't grow**. You may just think you're doing a good job. Get someone who can actually give you some valuable feedback and help you develop your techniques.

Quite often if an instructor gets negative feedback, they'll generally brush it off as, oh what do they know, they don't know what they're talking about? In some instances that could be true, but if you keep getting the same negative feedback and you want to improve then you've got to have a look at why you I keep getting this?

Then ask somebody, can you come and watch me and tell me about **this area** of feedback I'm getting. Your observer may say yes, you do talk very, very fast. Or you did say "obviously" 27,000 times.

The Singing Instructor

I've got a little story around that one. It was many years ago when I first started instructing. There was a guy, a regiment friend of mine, and he was teaching weapons, the various parts of a weapon. It was the days of the OHT, (overhead transparencies), you had to draw them yourself, then you put them on the OHP (Overhead Projectors) and you switched on the screen and talked about it.

That was your visual aid. I was observing him, (at his request), and he put the slide on and then when he went to press the button to light the slide up he'd go, **der derdle ler der derrr(singing)** and press the light button, and the light would come on, and the picture would be up on the wall. He did that every single time he pressed the button; he went **(de derdle ler der derrr)**. After the lesson he asked me what I thought? I said, "well the lesson was really good, the information's fantastic but you're doing something that I don't think you know about."

He says, "Well what is it?
I said, "Well tell me what you do when you put the overhead projector slide on?"

He said, "Well there's a cut out in the top right-hand corner, so I make sure that goes to the top right-hand corner. I also make sure I've told them what they're going to see, so it's not unexpected. Then I lay it down, and I press the button, and the light comes on and the picture is illuminated up on the screen."

I said, "You do all of those things and the picture does go up on the screen, except for just before you press the button you sing. **Der Derdle ler Der Derrr!**"

He said, 'oh my God do I really?'

I said, "Yes you do. This is how many times you've done it," and I showed him the piece of paper where I'd made a tally of every time he had sung **Der Derdle ler Der Derrr!"**

He wasn't aware he was doing it. He was doing a good lesson apart from that. What do you think the students remembered? Oh, he's the guy who sings, the presenter who sings a little tune just before he turns on the overhead projector. It's really important to know what you are doing, what effect you as a trainer are having on the students.

The Respected Peer Review Form found on the next page can be downloaded at BRIAN8.com.

Respected Peer Review Form.	
(Observations on YOU not the content of the lesson)	
VOICE: - Tone, Pitch, Speed, Volume, Intonation.	
EYES: - Blinking, looking where, catching the gaze.	
HEAD: - Nodding, Shaking, Wobbling (Agreeing, disagreeing, unsure)	
TORSO: - Facing audience, posture	
ARMS: and LEGS Too much, too little, fidget, same old repeat. Crossed, in pocket. Tapping bouncing.	
LANGUAGE: - Layman's, Technical, Jargon, TLAs (Three Letter Abbreviations)	
ATTIRE: - How do they look? Smart Scruffy, Too smart even?	
ODOUR: - Do you need a minty? If no one ever has the courage to tell you. You may be having an unwanted effect on your students.	

CHAPTER SEVEN

TIPS AND TRICKS FOR PRESENTING

Engage your audience with the right language

You've got to stay positive, think about the language that you are using. If you're going to engage your audience and they're all rocket scientists then you need to learn rocket scientist language. But if they're not rocket scientists and you start talking rocket scientist language, you're going to miss them completely.

You need to think about the way that you are engaging, and the words you're using. Some people may be from different countries, speak different languages, have different cultures and a different take on what you're saying. Think about slowing down and being aware of the effect that you may be having.

Years ago, when I was training to be an aerobics instructor, (yes, I became an aerobics instructor for a short while). I'd just done a weight training instructors course for three weeks prior, so I had a lot of knowledge in my head.

I asked a lot of questions and contributed greatly to discussions. At the end of the course the female instructor informed me that I had passed the course and she also offered me a position at a training event she was working at. Then she said to me "but first I need to tell you something that you're probably not aware of."
I said, "Well what's that then?"

She says, "I've written it down so you can read it and better understand it." and then she read it to me and it said,

"Brian Ward; needs to let people get to know him for two to three weeks before he unleashes the full potential of his personality upon them."

"You're scaring some people to death, with your knowledge and passion for this subject and your enthusiasm."

This happens to a lot of trainers. I've recently observed this in the last few weeks with a trainer who was teaching a group of executive leaders.

A really passionate and knowledgeable guy but presenting to the audience in a one-way delivery style, with passion and speed, it came across as push, push, push. He thought he was engaging. Unfortunately, he was pushing people away.

When you do get excited about your subject, your voice changes, your tone changes and you may not realise it. Your tone goes up a level and so does your volume. You may start to come across as intense when really you are just passionate.

It may sound like you're telling people off. let them see a little bit of your passion but be mindful of your tone.

I used to have a little note above the telephone and it just read, "T.O.T.P." Someone asked is that "Top of The Pops" (wow showing my age now) I said "no it's to remind me of my Tone on The Phone."

If you're trying to develop yourself practice with your family, friends and people around you. Sometimes when I'm talking to my wife, she may say to me, "Tone", and we know that it's just her little way to remind me that I do have a tone and I need to turn it down and make it good.

Some ways to practice this are when you're out and about, going to petrol stations and shops, engage with people.

Talk to people and try to listen to your own voice. It doesn't just develop or happen naturally; you have to practice these things.

Acknowledge your audience

It's really important that when we engage with our audience we find out where they are and we support learning at their level. Just take it easy and begin to get to know who your audience are.

There are some practical ways that people can acknowledge their audience in a really positive way.

If you have people in the room who are knowledgeable in the subject acknowledge them. I did a presentation once about safety in shopping centres around Active Threat (nasty people with guns) and there was a policeman at the back of the class.

He'd been a policeman for 20 years, and I knew he was just observing, so I made a point of acknowledging him, "I'd just like to say today we've got Peter at the back of the class, Peter has been a policeman for 20 years, has been involved with a lot of the things that we're going to talk about. So we might drop a few questions onto Peter later, if that's okay with you Peter?"

Peter, "Oh yeah that's fine, that's good, thank you." I'm acknowledging the expertise in my class. Then I'd also say but it's okay if you know nothing about this subject, 'because that's why we are here. You're just saying, it's okay we are all here to learn. Acknowledging that people are at all different levels of knowledge is really important.

Ask them what they want

Creating buy-in for people is all about them, here's a great set of questions that I found 20 years ago in a book called "Transactional Analysis for Trainers" by Julie Hay. The questions are used for contracting purposes (buy in) and have always worked well for me.

1. What do **you** want from this course?
2. How will **you** know when you have got it?
3. What are **you** prepared to do to get it?
4. What might stop **you** from getting it?
5. What might sabotage **your** chances of success?

Sometimes I will get the students to write each answer down on separate post-it notes and post them on a board with the words, Want, Know, Do, Stop and Sabotage. They simply stick them over the corresponding words.

I offer some encouragement by saying "it's all about what you want, not me, not your boss, not your parents or your friends. But what do you actually want from this training?

Once the board is full of post-it's a quick review helps set the tone of the training.

Keeping It Real

One of the key things you can do is, what I call keeping it real. Creating an environment where it's okay for people to ask the things that they want to ask, without the fear of being ridiculed.

Here's a little story on that one, I was sitting on an airplane once. It was a small aircraft with two rows of seats down each side. The pilot said, "look team we've got a problem with the toilets at the back, there's a sensor that's not working, so we're thinking of just not using the toilets and we'll fly on. Is that okay with everybody?"

Everybody was really silent, but it was awkward. It wasn't okay with me, and I said, "excuse me I'd just like to say that," I leant forward into the cockpit, "I'm an ex aircraft engineer and I'm not happy with flying on an aircraft where somethings not working. "He said, "No sir, you're exactly right," and we all got off.

As we got off the gentleman next to me said, "I'm really glad you said something." Because I wanted to say something but didn't feel confident in the environment, because of the way the message was put across.
That Aircraft didn't fly anywhere that whole day!

Get Creative

Here are a couple of ideas that can help presenters really take it to the next level. Exploration is a good thing, so watch what other people are doing. Get out and about and see what's out there.
Search the internet for games and activities, there is an important difference between a game and an activity. a

game is just a game. It's something to do, it's entertaining, but if you can make your game become an activity then it's really worthwhile doing.

I once had to deliver a lesson on suspicious parcels. I had a group of people at a naval base and we did a suspicious parcel activity. I created this activity.
Rather than me telling them what a suspicious parcel looked like. I made two identical suspicious parcels, they had too many stamps on, grease marks, wires sticking out, unevenly weighted, the address was spelt wrong and a few more issues.

I split the group in two and positioned each team either side of a white board. "I'm going to give you an envelope and I'd like you to write on the white board all the things you think are suspicious about the envelope. The winning team is the one who has the most observations. You have got two minutes". It was an activity where people got involved, and they communicated to each other in their teams.

They wrote their observations on their side of the board and then we discussed and expanded on their findings as a whole group.

With a bit of thought I created a fun, engaging and educating activity

The presenter

You are the most important element. If you don't look good, smell good and move good, you won't get your message across. How do you look and sound to your audience?

Self-Reflection

Take the time to look in the mirror first thing in the morning before you go and put yourself in front of other people.

I've seen so many presenters who have failed to take notice of their own appearance and grooming. Nose hair is unsightly, as is lots of ear hair, dandruff on your shoulders this does not inspire people to listen to what you are saying. Body odour, bad breath, wrinkled clothing, scruffy shoes etc., all take away from your credibility as a presenter, trainer or facilitator.

Next let's look at the words that you're using, the knowledge you've got, the experiences.

Is too much coming out of you? Are all the stories your stories? Are you talking too much?

Have you built pauses into your activities, into your day?

Quite often I will pause and I'll say, "okay team I've been talking for 10 minutes I just want you to talk to the person next to you, just for 15 seconds, talk about one thing that you've picked up so far."

Then I'll shut up, this also gives me a chance to look down at my notes, reflect on how I'm coming across to the audience, reflect on how the audience is buying-in to the training and have I covered what I wanted to over on that period.

Then when I'm ready (which may be a bit longer than 15 seconds) I'll just turn around and say, okay team where are we now and what have we talked about?

Draw the information from the class. That gives you a chance in the lesson to be aware of yourself too.

When they are engaged with somebody else; you can have a quick reflection on yourself. Is this good, is that good? Does that work all right? Constantly self-assessing and giving yourself a little bit of space within the presentation is really important.

Pace, speed of delivery, and how you are actually moving about the class is really important too. It's good not be rooted to the spot.

A lot of people do get stuck to a lectern or stand behind a desk and think that's where they have to stay. When I was in the armed forces, I taught presentation skills to senior staff. They would often insist on standing behind the lectern and simply reading the information.

No, No, No, get out from the lectern, put your hand in your pocket, relax, you're a human not a robot, move around, be a real person, engage with people.

Storytelling

The power of stories to transmit information and how you can adapt your stories, will accelerate learning and create high impact training.

If you can put things into a story it makes it so much easier, because it follows a logical sequence and people can remember a story rather than a bunch of facts. But if you can make the story relate to their situation. For example, if you are teaching about safety, you're talking about a real safety event that may have happened in their area where they work.

Not some fictitious thing that you made up or heard about that doesn't affect them whatsoever. Stories are fantastic, make them real, and if possible, use their stories.

If you say has this happened to anybody here? And somebody has an example ask them "Would you mind sharing that with us today?" People are quite often quite happy to share something with the rest of the class. And if they are not then that's OK you can still use a story of your own.

Hairy Dog Story

Now sometimes a story can go on too long and lose the point. When I train trainers, I spend some time observing them and I have listened to some fantastic stories. But often the story was much more interesting and went so far away from the topic that we forgot what the topic was.

It needs to be relevant, a story should be interesting, short, to the point, and it's just another analogy of what could have happened. Not a whole story where people remember the story and remember nothing else. That's what we call a hairy dog story where the story goes off in so many different directions, we just don't know what the point was in the first place. So avoid the hairy dog stories. Keep your story relevant, keep it short, keep it to the point and stay on track.

Owning it

There's a couple of tips that I believe every presenter needs to know about taking ownership of their presenting style, and getting feedback. You've got to be in the right place, you've got to want to inspire and engage.

Presenting's not something you do to make money, presenting's something you do because you really enjoy being out there, and if you don't then you should start to enjoy it, because it's a great vocation.

Think about, am I set up, am I ready, am I smiling, am I enjoying myself?

Quite often I work off a mind map, if you've not seen a mind map before, it's a sheet of paper with drawings and a few words here and there, it's a basic lesson prep. You can just glance down and see where you're supposed to be, instead of trying to read through a whole pile of words. Having mind maps can really keep you on track; they can keep you in a good place.

Here's an example of one of my mind maps.

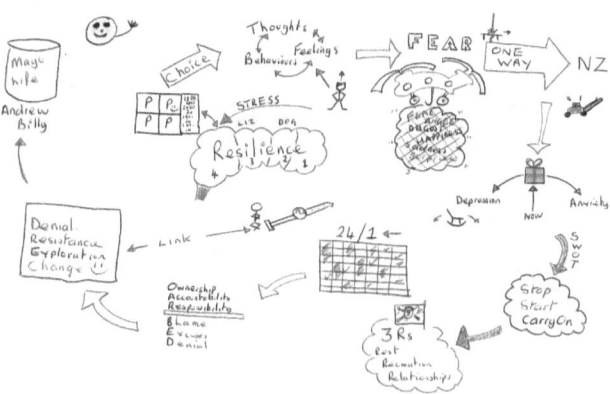

Props

Having some props in the classroom will help you accelerate the learning. A ball for instance, many times I've used a soft hand sized football for getting to know people's names. "I'm just going to throw the ball towards you, can you catch that, tell me your name, and then throw it back. It's just something, it's a movement, it allows people to move, then everybody starts to engage, oh I better get ready I don't want to drop it. It switches people on. Then the next person you throw it to ask them to "throw it to anybody you like, and let's get their name" Now you've taken yourself out of it and they're running the group themselves. A little bit of fun, a little bit of laughter, and not too risky but pretty much setting the scene for, hey, it's not too scary.

If you go in there and you start juggling straight away or doing something stupid that doesn't fit, you've gone too mad. Start off nice and easy, Start involving the group, get things happening for you.

Self-Aware

Becoming a self-aware presenter is really one of the most important elements of this whole process, because when you become a self-aware presenter you become able to improve on your own.
You're gathering feedback, you're assessing that feedback, and you're developing and having a much greater impact on the people that you're training.

You'll have the skill to self-reflect, it's happening while you're doing a lesson, but it's also happening afterwards too. Through asking other people what you were like, and taking a bit of time out for yourself to think, how did that go? Did that go like I wanted it to go? Is there anything I could have improved? If you have that chat with yourself first, then when you talk to the person who's giving you feedback you can think, yes, that's what I thought too. There's that confirmation that I need to develop a bit more. No matter what you think you're doing, you have an effect on your audience, let's have the best effect we can, let's have a positive effect.

Remember the three things that are really important to increasing the impact of your training are: -

- Engage your audience.
- Create an inspiring learning environment.
- Understand how to grow and develop you.

CHAPTER EIGHT

HOW TO GET MORE HELP?

If I've inspired you with my creativity and you would like help and assistance becoming the best trainer you can be,

please contact me at brian8@trainandmotivate.com.au or for more information on lessons from BRIAN8 visit brian8.com.

Or even call me on 0413575 876,
I'm a pretty easy-going guy and I don't bite.

Now go and have some fun

Lessons and Workshops from BRIAN8

- Presenter Training
- Reflection and Feedback
- Accelerated Training Techniques
- Conflict Resolution
- Time Management
- Inspiring Through Story Telling
- Change Management
- Advanced Facilitation
- Leadership

- How to utilise a Mind Map
- Engaging Your Audience
- Laughter in Learning
- Practical Activities

www.ingramcontent.com/pod-product-compliance
Lightning Source LLC
Chambersburg PA
CBHW030454010526
44118CB00011B/931